under the skin of the world

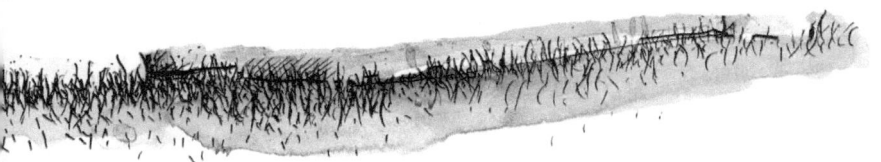

under the skin of the world

Zoe Anderson

Drawings by Helani Laisk

RECENT WORK PRESS + AMPERSAND DUCK

contents

vii   *preface*

mountains

- 3   Frost Hollow
- 7   The Catchment
- 10   Wild Horses
- 13   The Stone Witch
- 25   Erasing Geography
- 29   These are Dull Steal Days
- 33   Cleopatra

back across the valley

- 41   Time Makes Deserts
- 44   Breathe
- 45   Driving Straight Through
- 47   All Over the Floor
- 52   Their Summer Call

from the ashes

- 57   Enough Filthy Mutants
- 58   Recipe for Fire (Again)
- 60   Unwelcome Warmth
- 61   Voices
- 66   Feather Down

69   *notes*
70   *about us*

preface

When I started writing these poems, it was imagining a future that I could dimly perceive. One that I hoped would not come to pass. Working on the publication of this book throughout the horrors of the 2019/2020 national bushfire crisis has made this collection feel almost like a relic of the past. An artefact from when we were just speculating about a new future under climate change. For many of us, that future is now here. For many others of course, the realities of climate change have been present for some time. Perhaps it's helpful to take a measure of these rolling waves of shifting reality as they break over the uneven shoreline of our communities.

Some of the poems in this collection are from when I first started writing seriously – about eight years ago. At the time it felt like art about climate change was a small niche, now it feels like a dominant theme in much of the art I come across. I'm glad that we're finding new ways to talk and think about the future of this planet. For me, writing about planetary change has been all about finding these new ways, making the discourse more accessible, less scary. Let it become part of our lexicon, our language, our mental shorthand, our patterns of thought about the world.

For as long as I've had the capacity to reflect, I've seen the world through this lens of climate change. It's not always a comfortable vantage point to occupy, but it's an awful lot less lonely, less scary when there are other people sharing it. I hope we can continue to make stories about the orchids we see sprouting in the burnt-out forests.

Zoe Anderson, February 2020

mountains

frost hollow

stand here
and see
the landscape
a bowl
cold air falls
sinks down to pool in
hollow, in mist, in frost
the crisp air amassed. this
is where the snowgums grow.

stand still.
this place
its tip touches
deep time.
this stand
of trees
gave birth to trees
this stand
stood here
since
each tree reaches
back
to the last ice age.

back to the land
here, whole,
cold, crowned
with snowgums.

hear the roar
of cars along

the interchange
the meeting of four
arterial highways
a crossroads.

she comes to the frost hollow
each time
she has to make a choice
in life

to stay, to go
to take the leap of faith.
decisions based on heart
or hope or health.

she takes her question to
the snowgums
to the crossroads
to the traffic's constant stream.
to the everchanging
immutability
of the trees.

she was born in the crisis
she grew up playing in erosion gullies.
never known grasslands
that weren't deflated, overgrazed.
she was born in the middle
or perhaps the end
lived so much of her life in drought
the sound of rain makes her nervous
a tap that's been left to run.

she was born in the crisis
and she cannot chose to leave the crisis
and she doesn't know what to do
unable to form a question
decisions in this crisis seem
futile, thin, unclear

all she can do is
stand here
and see
the landscape
a bowl
cold air falls
sinks down to pool in
hollow, in mist, in frost
the crisp air amassed –

all she can do is
stand still.
this place
its tip touches
deep time.
this stand
of trees
gave birth to trees
this stand
stood here since-
each tree reaches
back to-
an ice age.

all the way back
to the land
here, whole,
cold, crowned
with snowgums.

the catchment

On these hot nights
Sleep doesn't come
till hours after sunset.
She lies in bed with the hum
of the fan standing sentry.
Has to wake every hour
to drink water.

She imagines all the moisture
slowly leaving her body
Imagines herself drying
becoming smaller,
lighter, her body gaining
wrinkles in its shrinking
Everything in her evaporated
to a dry husk by dawn.

She imagines all the moisture
slowly leaving this land.
Puddles, ponds, creeks, rivers disappearing
wetlands and swamps becoming
ashy, brittle, gone.

She tosses in the living, hot night,
casts her mind upstream
to the catchment,
lucky land left uncleared
left alone to flourish.
Bush scrub acts as sponge and earthmat,
filters rainfall, holds shallow soil together.

Watershed:
sharp curve of ridgelines
determines where each drop will run,
flows to creaks, to swamps
filters ever downwards
towards wide walled dams.

The night is bloated,
baked with lack of sleep.
She drives out of town
follows winding roads
across narrow bridges.
Leaves the car,
climbs a fire trail
step by steep step.

In the cool dawn she stands
above the broad built wall.
Eyes roam over flat fastness
over safe stored gigalitres.

As if absorbing moisture
she feels her body relax
Sure of this one thing

For now.

wild horses

He said he didn't believe
their presence was causing absence
causing change.
Moss, delicate
water plants trampled
frogs and fish facing
extinction.
Loss of grasslands,
of small marsupials.
No proof he said.
He said the horse is from this place.
He said
their stories wearing tracks,
hard hooves cutting soft hillsides for
as long as he could remember.

And wild horses couldn't drag him
to make him change his mind.

Wild horses certainly couldn't
starving as they were
ribs showing
gagging for water.
Dumb instinct unable
to comprehend
a landscape ill adapted.

But next time he stood
among snow gums
among tussock grass,

a horde of small extinct mammals,
reptiles, amphibians,
rose up out of the ancient time
stored in those stark hard hills
and they dragged him
kicking and screaming,

dragged him
bloody and weeping
weeping then limp
till he had no mind to change.

Dragged him
who   knows   where

and the mountains will not say
and they will not change their mind.

the stone witch

This is the story
This is the story of how I fell
How I fell into the earth
How I fell into the earth under an almond orchard
The earth of small life and cold rock and damp rotting stone

In the autumn when the leaves are paper bag crackle
And the air is blue smoke
And the clean threat of frost.
Autumn is the time for almonds,
Rich seed from tree
To shell indoors on foggy mornings.
King parrots keyed their b flat call into the overcast
As I approached the almond tree.
Lazy I gave the laden limbs a shake
And out fell the Stone Witch
The Clay Witch, Tor Witch
Witch of mesa and canyon
She flies on the wind with dust and parna
And settles where it settles
A sedimentary witch
Born of parts and movement and the changing world.

The Stone Witch rose up
With a marzipan stink
    (She'd been eating unshelled almonds,
    They were stuck in her teeth)
And her wrath
Was a rock fall
A landslide
It didn't know borders, or fences
Or personal space

She said:
you!
Must learn patience
Patience of the earth
Patience of the mud and the rock and the rotting things.
> (Her fury and her bad breath were one,
> Rolling over me as hot brown fog.)

She said:
This tree has been turning air into soil
For longer than you've had all your molars.
It draws in sunlight
And turns it into almonds,
It feeds itself with fungi
And at the same time it feeds me.

do not
Shake the boughs and try to disrupt that process
Witches need nourishment too.

you will know my fury.

This is the story of how I tried to make peace
   with the Stone Witch
How I offered her a pot
Of smoked black tea
Opals and quartz
Kangaroo bones and echidna quills

But the Stone Witch did not want these things.

you will learn patience

She knocked the disposable coffee cup from my hand

you will learn patience

She crushed my phone beneath her feet

you will learn patience at the speed of geology

Patience is the sound of continents colliding
And when you have learnt it

you will no longer bother me

With your tree shaking ways.

This is the story of how the Stone Witch put me
into the earth.

How she picked up five almonds
And she threw them
And before they landed
I was under the ground.

And the ground was cold, and the ground was full of life,
Roots running everywhere like the arteries of a city.
Mould and bacteria, arthropods and worms
Ceaselessly eating dirt and dead leaves and fungi.
Mycelium wreathing a root system in wedding veil white,
Hyphae spreading into the soil like lace.

But the Stone Witch had followed me down
And she leaned in close.
    (Her breath soaking, stinking, infiltrating.)
She said: don't touch the mycelium
It's not lace
It's busy doing useful work

Unlike you.

This mycorrhiza knows only this earth
And the roots of the tree that it clings to.
It feeds the roots,
And it tells the tree stories
Of all the feasting that goes on down below.

This fungi turns soil
Into food for trees and witches.
>(She chomped and gnawed on the fleshy white decay
>It did not improve her bad breath
>just changed the nature of it.)

And she said:
These fungi and bacteria breathe, they eat,
They fight and have children.
They worship the roots and the rock and the rain,
They never think to steal almonds from witches.

She said:
With one word, I could condemn you
To this small dark existence,
Getting upset over ants and excited over leaf mould,
But I said I'd teach you patience
And for that, we must go further.

The clay was heavy around my body,
The microbes were nibbling my toes
To see if I was dead and could be eaten yet.
I was scared, but I dared not say a word
That might anger the Stone Witch.
So I waited.

And with the changing of the seasons,
With seeping moisture and shifting warmth,
With flood and mud, deposition,
Silt and subsidence,
I was descending.
But infuriatingly slowly,
I was falling down.

This is the story of how the Stone Witch took me down.
Down through loam and humus and damp clay,
And heavy clay to bedrock,
The parent material.

The Stone Witch poked me in the ribs and said
Its proper name was *Regolith*.
I turned my head to avoid her fungus breath
And turned again
Where does soil end and rock begin?

Idiot

Said the witch
Everything rots, everything breaks down
Soils that are parented here
Are formed over millions of years
Rock disintegrates to clay, or sand, or silt
Through work that is not worth
Measuring through millennia
Measuring through flippant trips around the sun

you would give up, you would lose count ten thousand times
And ten thousand again and still the process would not be completed
Would not have made an ounce of soil.

I shuddered and said to the Stone Witch
Yes, I get it
These things take time
Lots of time.
Thanks for your trouble
Could you send me back now
I'm bored, and cold
And my clothes have rotted.

But the Stone Witch
Munched on silica until her teeth turned to granite.
She breathed on me
Her breath was worse than before,
And I dared not struggle.
I had no way to measure the time that was passing.
The cold that was seeping
The minerals rotting.

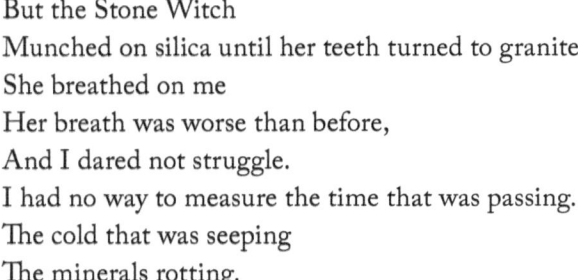

And the silence.
And the pressure.

And as I lay,
There, under the earth
I began to disintegrate.
cell by cell,
flesh decayed,
i watched it
cold sedateness
rock dissolved
like water and salt,
stirred to liquid
flowing, but containing
solid stone within.

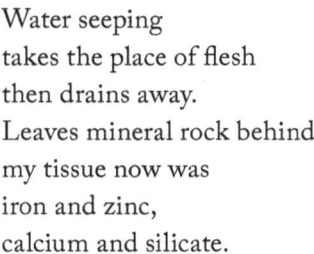

Water seeping
takes the place of flesh
then drains away.
Leaves mineral rock behind
my tissue now was
iron and zinc,
calcium and silicate.

And when my bones had lithified
Completely
I could not speak.
I tried to look at the witch
But my spine was hard, unmoving.
And she spat out some pebbles
She'd been eating
And said:

Not until the continents collide
And make this land anew
Will you learn patience.
I have had you fossilised,
Body turned to stone
So you can move at the pace
Of important things happening.
you will never shake an almond tree again
never steal from soil and stone.

She left me there,
A splinter lodged under the skin of the world.
She told me that very few fossils
get found by people.

She left me there,
No way to measure the time trickling in to fill the space
where my skin once was
She left me there
Turned to stone
and stone soon turned to acceptance.

As around me, the stones started speaking
Telling me their dreams of the future
Telling me how this was not the end

How through erosion and time and perhaps tectonics
The minerals we were made of
Would rise to the surface
Feel the warmth of the sun
And the hum of life
And be eaten, absorbed
Passed from microbe to tree root
Sap, bark, leaves...

The stones told me that someday
Some of them might cling to carbon dioxide
    falling from the atmosphere
And drag it deep into the ocean,
Where it will be turned in to sea shells, and crab claws
    and urchin spines.

The stones told me that if I was lucky
I would sink down into the warm heart of the earth
Embraced by magma and there made new.

As I lay there, still and stone
I lost count of the futures the rocks laid out before us
Lulled into a sense of oneness
Faded into being part of something bigger
Neither impatient or kind.

Part of an oldness in in its entirety crumbling into other processes
Part of a system both wholly of this minute and so ancient
As to be wordless no name
Needed for something
That's always been there, always will
On any timescale worth measuring.

Through millimetres and centuries the rocks moved,
And I knew rebirth, renewal and eternal fiery dawn
A slow forever remaking, endless incorporation, accretion, acceptance
Everything and everything buried and uncovered and forever being
And being made

Witch and rock
Soil and body and microbe
Always unbecoming
All sense of injustice, forgiveness, anger
Folded and faulted into ancient conglomerations

This is the story
This is the story of how I fell
How I fell in to the earth
How I fell in to the earth and acceptance and unmeasured time
Small life and huge rock and damp, rotting stone. Became
Grit, dust, crystal,
A sedimentary witch
Born of parts and movement and the changing world
Moments uncounted, unlooked for
No sense of loss, no loss of home

erasing geography

She is the deity of all
highway rest stops.
Like a patron saint but ambiguous,
she eats plastic bags
as offerings. Picnic table
her alter, her name is unpronounceable
but you can hear it in the shuddering scream
of a semi trailer's
compression braking.

She has her own script
this deity of the in-between places
her own way of writing
it is the curling looping scrawl
of tyre marks, branded
over empty carpark lines.

Each swipe of a blowfly
is a gesture of reverence
to the deity of highway rest stops.
As you enter the long drop dunny
do not inhale, do not
look behind you
you are not alone
she is in there with you
she is in every
uncomfortable brown mark
every stain
on wall and floor.

Only the deity of highway rest stops
can engineer the kind of argument
that you get
trapped
in a speeding metal box
travelling between cities.

And when you pull over
to cool off
the place you stop
is no place at all.
Cigarette butts are the same,
you've seen that man
pissing in the bushes before

Or one like him
You forget your arguing
this place is no-where
made into nothing.

Flinch at some wad
of stained tissue in the bushes,
surreptitiously leave your rubbish
next to the overflowing bin.
Do not see
the grove
of fern and tea tree
over barbed wire fence.

You pray to her
each time you say the phrase
in the middle of nowhere
you pray to her.

This place is a microcosm
inside a vacuum
a world unto itself
a bead
on the string
of the highway.

Combustion engine roar
erasing geography
there is nothing between
but patchy reception
and someone's fast food feast
strewn on the pavement
by seagull, or ibis.
The deity of highway rest stops
she squats down and
eats with them
and when the birds die
of plastic
twisted
around their insides
she eats their bodies also
carries their souls
over

the highway
that roars
on and on
drivers knowing only
that they're passing nowhere
journeys measured in tyre tread
in bottles of coke
in the rim of a Styrofoam cup
in tanks of petrol
measured in the distance between phone charges
in device battery life
in the size of the dark patches between signal.

Waiting is another form of connection
the giving and receiving of attention.

The highway roars
on and on
gives her form, a presence
in nowhere

these are dull steal days

There's some out there'd say these is fallen times.
dogs are vicious and librarians roam rampant,
launching gang warfare pon any poor soul
fool enough to touch the precious printed word with bare hand.

These is felled-forest, meat-rot dead-root times,
iron ore oil stain sky times,
bushfires ain't something that's fought.
fire's coming – yer get the hell out of the way.

These is broken-down days,
ain't no road workers, no street lights.
no sewage treatment plants, no police force,
ain't no goddamn bus network.
territory and municipal services
a fairy story,
whispered at firesides,
Macarthur House long since become an anti-cyclist squat.

Lightrail? buried underneath tar and leaf litter,
rolling stock become
glasshouses and incubation systems. closely guarded.
no fool dare approach.
in these dull steel blunt instrument times
there's one thing folk count on.
one thing to set a watch for:

The garbage collectors.
no one knows how they power their trucks.
rumoured they'd converted to nuclear
back in the methane wars of '68,
errything ends up in the tip eventually,

the garbos' union's arm stretches long
as a Hitachi digger.
pressure like a compactus.
nothing gets past a bulldozer's claws.

No one knows why they do it.
'cept it stands to reason like. Stop collecting garbage
and you aint a garbo no more.
nothing more 'lectrifying
than spotting a team of them, powersuited
in overalls. out on a bin run.
hunting down the green tubs.
stuffing the truck.

And the people holed up in their little cold houses
whisper to each other in the damp dark:

> *put your bins out*
> *put your bins out*
> *put your bins out*

Nowadays, folks know better than to
show disrespect to a garbo. word got around
'bout someone didn't sort his 'cyclables.
glass bottles in
with the plastic bags.

Big truck seen in front of his place at midnight.
men in overalls carrying shovels.
muffled screaming and thumps.
high pressure hose.
hydraulic lift.

never heard from him again.

put your bins out
    put your bins out
        put your bins out

Garbage men's pits are deep,
their resources pile stinking and infinite.
hot compost system they've got out there
can break down a carcass in 48 hours.

put your bins out

Some folks'd say the garbage men
are the best thing going for us.
come to your home every week and take away
things you don't need.
the smelly, and bulky, the ugly, embarrassing,
sharp and dripping, dank unwanted offensive.
they'll carry it away.
they'd say them's the last thing as
keeps us from living in filth.

Vermin is rampant, the last
hospital went under other day,
doctors live in secret cos they 'fraid
of being mobbed,
too many among us are sick,
injured, dying,
drains and sewers blocked up long ago,
running water something people joke about.

'cept the streets are clean.
No litter is ever seen
round here
consequences of that are worse'n death.

all folks have to do is follow the sanctified order of the green
and yellow lids. rinse yer containers.
bag up your rubbish

put your bins out

put your bins out

put your bins out

Cleopatra

There was this princess, *Cleopatra*
Who got bitten by an adder
In a tower, had a slumber,
Earth rotations without number

The *snake*, he was no wicked fairy,
Just a reptile who was fairly
Furious to be mistaken
For some spindle, he was trying
To sell fruit to turn a living

The point is that he pierced her finger
And she felt extremely *sleepy*
In a tower in Belconnen
Made her bed, she'd washed the linen
Cleaned her teeth and drew the curtains
Though she'd left the window open
Taken out her contact lenses,
Put her phone upon the nightstand
Closed her eyes and started *dreaming*

There followed year-in year-out sleeping
While *the wind it blew* the curtains
'till they tattered into ribbons

And she didn't stir or waken
As her tower, *struck by lightning*
So the roof, it cracked right open
And *the rain*, it trickled sometimes
When it wasn't *snow* or *sleeting*
(It's the future, there's shit weather)

And time was measured in the meanwhile
Between the *sleeting storms* and *bushfires*
In the hills above Belconnen
No one left was counting decades
'cos *hurricanes* don't know high numbers
And *the rain* decayed the bedclothes
And the carpet and the floorboards
Made them soft and wet and spongy
So that mould and mites and fungi

Found their way into the tower
Where they drank up the rainwater

Then an apple in the corner
Left abandoned by the adder
Felt the life that was beneath it
Split and sprouted, shoots and tendrils.

Meanwhile,

Cleopatra, she was *sleeping*
She was *dreaming*, she was *breathing*
And beneath her broken ceiling
All her jet black hair was *growing*,
Overflowing off the pillow
Over floor and out the window
Past the swiftly *sprouting* seedlings
Who'd brought friends, small leafy green things
Fine laced roots like fingers, *feeling*
Seeking anything to hold to.
Slow and tender like a lover
mil by mil they did discover,
Weave with skill like blind bone mother
Fine white roots and crow black hair

Soon, hair twisted around branches
Vines grabbed onto it for purchase
And of course, as nests for birds.

Four-score years passed in Belconnen
'till one hurricaning morning

☞ *The Lady Kim, Urban Explorer* ☜
Dropped with a cry her best machete
Stared with pure ungarnished *wonder*
At this woman of the forest
Hair a cloud of fine black tangles
Filaments in branch and bramble
Fingernails of moss and mottle
Stains from rain and leaves leave bottle
Greenish blotches on her visage
Kim stared and stared, for *longest* moment

But then a lisping in the corner
Sounded just like '*kiss, kiss, kiss her*'

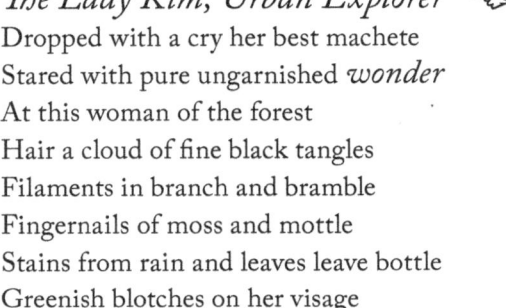

Some part of Kim just *longed* to wake her
Kiss her gently, hold her, ask her
How it felt to be so truly
Soil and forest, leaf and fungi

Then Kim had another vision
Sleeping woman, waking *screaming*
Hair all torn from scalp and seedling
No more at peace, but stuck between
A forest and a human being

So *Lady Kim, Urban Explorer*
She laid down her best machete
And her wrist guards, on the nightstand
Took one look past curtains, creepers

To the hurricane, still raging
Turned away from planet's aging,
Fruitless cry, instead towards the
Place where Princess still lay sleeping
Cradled there by bough and fern frond
Kim lay *gently* down beside her
Knew in time the forest's growth would
Wind around her body *also*
Bound beside the sleeping woman

Kim *smiled* because they were *together*
In a forest, in a tower
In Belconnen, burnt and windblown
There would stay this sleeping story

The forest, with its shade and secrets
Grew to fill another day.

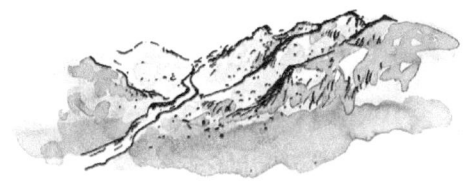

back across the valley

time makes deserts

Once there was a glassblower
A little bubble of a man
Whose lover died she bowled him over
Slipped away, was cold and stillness
Ashes scattered on the land
She loved and
Yearned for, sung for
Turned for
From a spry old thing
To ash for
Campaigned against the mines they dug there
Shouted at the barricades.

The stress and worry took this woman
Squeezed her out and left her dried up
Like an old gum, twisted, trying
To reflect the burning sun.

And grief and loss had made the old man's
Furnace dark for half a year
Lonely tears uncounted
Mounted melted into crumpled fears.

And now and then a visitor would knock and call
    and ask for glass
But door stayed shut and silent while inside
        the old man was a mess
He couldn't see the value in his art now that
        his love was dead
She fought for life and what was right and now
        he couldn't see the point
Of making glass if all around the world was falling

Choking slowly, dulling, darkening,
  facing its own self destruction
Why make beauty, all for naught.

Till one bright day there came a young man
Eyes of water hands a knocking
At the house of old glassblower
Called like smoke outside his door.

The young man said he'd lost his mother,
Felt emptiness inside his bones
And nothing really felt like home
But maybe if some glass was blown
Ballooned and round and floated down
The river like a bubble like a message in a bottle
Like a call just to remember her
And could the glass man please somehow
Make a big globe full of hope?

And as the old man heard this call
He rose and started work once more
And memories of his love were left
With every breath inside the glass

That soon would smash and crumble
Into shards and fragments, splinters, sand
As time makes deserts of the cities,
Forests, mountains, shops and mines.

Last night the old man and the young
They stood together
By the water,
Floated glass globes down
Upon the river
Like a bubble
Like a message in a bottle
Like a call though not for help
But for all of life
Just to remember.

Because all things will return to sand
But in the meantime, just sometimes
They can be seen as beautiful.

breathe

We share this apartment, a sink and a window
A bookcase, a kettle, no rug on the floor.
Two bedlamps, two laptops, toothbrushes, two housekeys
A deadlock and chain on the door.

I shoplift from Woolworths, you find food in dumpsters
I smoked your tobacco, you drank all my wine.
I read all your novels, you read all my poems
We both paid your speeding fine.

You chipped my last teacup, I lost half your chess set
You let my plants die when I went out of town.
You like to rise early, I can't stand the mornings,
If I'm up, you're just coming down.

You kissed all my workmates, I fucked all your school-friends
You don't like my mother, I pissed off your aunt.
You don't show for days, then brought home two girls
While I sat in the bath and read Kant.

Soon as the shops shut, we run out of condoms
You ripped my best stockings that time on the couch.
As nights threaten winter we nest in the doona
Curled up like two kits in a pouch.

I can't stand your cooking, you hate all my music
You mess up the kitchen, I scratch your CDs.
Unspoken agreements for spoken discussions
No Nietzsche, and no refugees.

You won't come to bed, and I won't call to ask you
But then in the morning you won't let me leave.
We circle each other, I inhale, you exhale,
Half full and half empty, we breathe.

driving straight through

sometimes
you've got to drive
all night. straight through,
stopping only to switch. Sometimes
falling in love is hard like bitumen and you've
got to take a good long look at the roadkill before deciding
that if it happens, it's worth it. and reach across
the gearstick and grab your lover's hand
before staring through the windscreen
focus on the middle distance
put your foot down
all the way   all the way,
                              in the backseat, arms
                              tangle with underwear, bras
                         & shoes. sometimes you forget to use
                  an indicator, to look before you turn. sometimes
            everything nearly falls out the window, snapped off
      like both your wing mirrors. the road stares back. it is two
broken headlights blankly pointing out just how fast you're
               travelling how far you've still to go. you rise to
                         the bitumen like a challenge, take their
                                   hand across the gearstick
                                        put your foot down
                                              all the way

all the way
watch the full moon
travel its skypath course as
you eat up kilometres with hours
until it rests on the horizon ahead.
take your lover's hand all the way and put
your foot down. drive until the moon is
roadkill. shattered across the highway
like two broken wing mirrors. you've
made a hole for your car to fit
through. take their hand
across the gearstick.
put your foot down
all the way

all over the floor

The tap in the bathroom was doing it
                                              too
   running white
               and bright,
        effervescing ever so slightly.
The stuff that came out didn't drain
                    down the plug hole.
The stuff that came out
         was floating,
               like *smoke*, like *steam*,
                    like when clouds come down
                    to mask Black Mountain

The tap in the garden was doing it
              pale milked and
                 pooling at ankle height all over the lawn.
The kitchen sink had overflowed
          the same stuff
                        like *liquid smoke.*

'Turn it off.'
I said,
'We probably shouldn't breathe it,
or ingest it
or whatever.'
'Let it run'
you said,
'It will probably
run clear by morning.'
I turned it off,
you turned it
back on.

I frowned and
you touched the
wrinkles on my forehead
said
I love you
in your way that means
stop frowning and let me be right,
please.
We went to bed
I closed all the doors
between the kitchen tap and us.
You slept.
I listened
to its pearly hiss and
thought of gas leaks, and
counted every breath.
Yours and mine.
It had not run clear by morning.

I got ready for work in a wading pool of *white*
                 s p r e a d   e v e n, all over the house.
'It whispers to my ankles'
you said.

I lost my shoes for a full ten minutes
and rushed out the door shouting
'will you please
turn the taps off now?
And call a plumber!'

That evening
   I followed a stream
      of *milk-smoke* home

You were lying in the bath
   naked,
      the cold *steamy-swirls* around you,
         running out of the tub
           and onto the tiles.

'Did-you-call-the-plumber?'
my words
were quiet,
compressed
by my lips
into thinness

You spiralled the white gas
                with your finger.
'Plumber said
he didn't know what was doing it
so he left again
his invoice is... somewhere round here.'

You
     started feeling under the mist
as I turned and walked out.

'I love you!'
You called
in your way that means
I'm sorry
           without actually being

                              sorry

The *ghostly smoke*
               waist deep now
You were singing
      In the bathtub as

I packed a bag,
found my shoes
again,
left as you were folding paper boats
   to sail
      on the opaque gaseous *whiteness*.

One,
the plumber's invoice,
   followed me down the hall
      out of the door,
         on the *dissipating mist*
           still pooling at my ankles,
as I stepped outside
into the clear,
   bright
    air.

their summer call

in the summer i will eat cicadas
brittle and juicy. red eyes
clear wings
until only their shells remain. dull
brown, hollow.
until my own voice is clicking and roaring with calls
calls across the hot dryness
for sex,
sex while the days are still warm.

in the autumn i will eat woodsmoke
from chimneys
and dried eucalyptus flowers.
my lover and i almost had a fight
in the blanketing cold darkness
and this morning we exchange music
and poems
via email. i refresh
the page
holding my smouldering breath.

in the winter i will eat the ghost of fireworks
and the cold
rocks of the brindabellas.
some days i retreat inside myself until
everyone is a stranger.
rocks sit in my stomach and hold me as
the winds send their snowy prayers down
to the city

and we look back, across the valley
for the abrupt white
for confirmation
of the cold

in the spring I will eat memories
i will eat floriade banners
i will eat capeweed
together we find ancient lines
for each day
we cannot stay out of the sun's new harsh embrace
i peel the first bloom of sunburn off your skin
and eat that as well

lying barefoot in the grass
and listening for the first cicada
i hope
that the turning of the world
doesn't kill their summer call

from the ashes

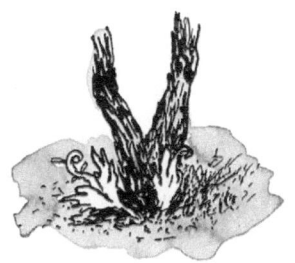

enough filthy mutants

And when my friend left a bag of meth here
we buried it in the garden
rather than flushing it down the toilet
because there's too much that ain't shit
in the sewage these days.

And when the frost came
there sprouted some thorny bush
that burst forth thistle flowers
that fruited into broken fingernails
and popped balloons.

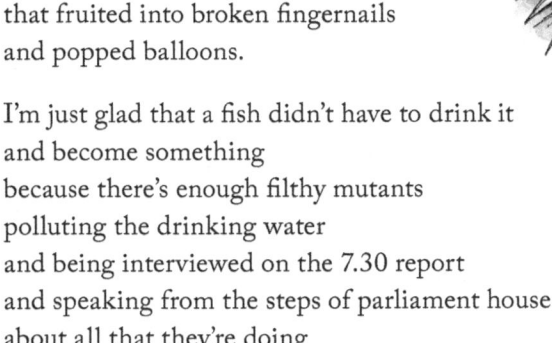

I'm just glad that a fish didn't have to drink it
and become something
because there's enough filthy mutants
polluting the drinking water
and being interviewed on the 7.30 report
and speaking from the steps of parliament house
about all that they're doing
to prevent us from losing our minds

especially if that's what we're trying to do.

And then he turns away from the cameras
adjusting his tie and walks quickly to the toilets
where he wretches and spews forth watery bile
containing broken fingernails and burst balloons
and thistledown

recipe for fire (again)

R: Something is on fire again
Z: He stands in the middle of the kitchen, armloads of pans, armloads of groceries, hands full of knives.
Z, R: Something is on fire again
Z: The air is wet with chopped onions
R: Even the knife is weeping
Z: The fan is on, the music is winding itself up to another breakdown in the next room and
Z, R: something is on fire again
Z: Eggs crack into bowls, run rivers of scramble foam, monsoon-yellow and thick enough to drown in. He stands in the middle of the kitchen and says:

R: I have lost my fish bones and my pork cutlets and my strawberries and my spoon. I accidentally have too many oysters and a Tiny Yotam Ottolenghi has climbed out of the cookery book and is screaming at me in a tiny passionate voice and –

Z, R: Something is on fire again

Z: Jerusalem artichokes mix freely with blood plums and soup. Carrots mutter to each other about what they have seen in the dark

R: Tiny Yotam Ottolenghi is spitting and hissing. He is the boiling oil that plots murder on the stove. Each chip submerged in its cholesteroline depths is carved in his sixinch image

Z: Yotam Ottolenghi is yelling tiny, well garnished abuse from the edge of the chip pan. He is throwing currants at the cook to catch his attention but –

R, Z: Something is on fire again

R: all I can find are these currants and three wheels of cheese. I swear I had several more strainers, and my vinegar has turned back into wine. I will mend this at once with digestives and pickled lemons, I will smother the situation in sriracha hot sauce and jam

Z: Tiny Yotam Ottolenghi spits tahini at the bookshelf, and makes a bold, arcane gesture with one tiny hand. Tiny Jamie Oliver and Tiny Nigella Lawson climb stiffly from the pages, uttering squeaky cries of abuse or applause, we will never know because –

Z, R: something is on fire again

R: and everywhere is anchovies. Anchovies in the jar, anchovies on the benchtop, anchovies on the floor, and my shoes, and my hair. What we need is more anchovies

Z: the thing that is happening on the stove top and bench is sandcastles in the sky, or hot blown glass in an ocean grotto, it is growing out of the kind of dream where you wake with the sheets drenched in sweat, it is growing and you cannot –

Z, R: look away

R: from this culinary juggernaut, this whisk- wielding thunder god, and you'll miss it,
Z: this mess in the making
R: this is no quiet, meditated act of creation. **This story**
Z, R: **is on fire again**
Z: This story is being told
Z, R: with a blender
Z: And no one is going to do the washing up
R, Z: Ever again

unwelcome warmth

Getting into the car, winter morning. So fucking early. All dark – just clouds, no sun. Getting into the car, winter morning: she pauses, because the insides of the windows are all fogged up. Fogged up like it's warm in there. Streetlights glare in the corner of her vision like an indictment, like a visual extension of the horror of the alarm clock still ringing in her ears. A magpie grumbles at the not-yet-morning, and a trickle of moisture runs down the driver's side window. She is still hesitating. All her senses tingle. But time is ticking and she didn't get up so damn early just to be late. She turns the key, slides into the driver's seat. All is quiet, and warm. Too warm. Without warning the door locks itself behind her. Something exhales in the gloom. Warm air on the back of her neck.

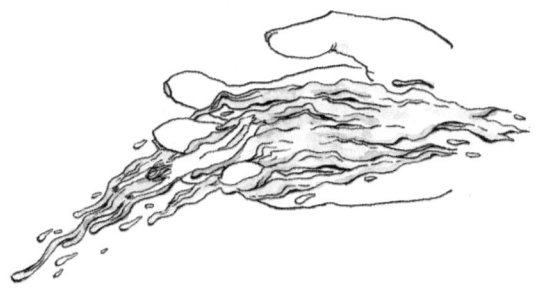

As the sun slowly finds its way into the world the car sits immobile in the driveway. The inside is invisible behind fogged windows. Nothing moves except a trickle of moisture running down the driver's side pane.

voices

All my life I have been looking.
I have been looking
For the castles in the clouds.
I have been looking
For the singing in the sunshine.
And the witches in the tea leaves.
And the face of jesus in the slice of potato.
I have been looking
For the source of the voices
The Voices that live inside of me
And tell me when not to do things.
When to shrink
And to run
And to be afraid.
These voices they are good to me, they know me best of all.

One day I found an accordion player
She had stripy stockings and her hair
Was held in place with a dagger
She said: the accordion is a rare beast
Inside each lives a hive of bees
You cannot let them get too hot
Or the wax inside will melt and run and stick
And the instrument will be ruined.
You cannot let them get too cold,
Or the bees inside will forget
The smell of summer
And turn to small grey pebbles
And your accordion will emit nothing but a sad death rattle.

She said: I am the accordion
And the accordion is me
I have to feed it with syrup
And blow pollen into its bellows every night
And I can never ever let it out of my sight
Because the bees are the only family I have now and families must look after each other.

I asked her about the voices inside of me,
And she said that she never heard things
like that anymore
Although she used to, a long time ago,
Before her accordion found her.

She offered to play a song for me and
Because the bees fly high
Over the rooftops
And can see many things
With their compound eyes
It just might show me my way.

The song spoke of a path
Written across the sky in sunshine
It spoke of daggers buried in hot wax
And feet dancing in bright stripy stockings.
I walked the way that the song told me to. Even though the voices said it wasn't worth it.

Next I found a man with some rocks
He had five that would fit into his fingers,
And he was throwing them to the ground
And recording precisely where each one fell.
Each time they fall it is different, he said.
And yet their relation to each other and to me
Is but a fleeting spark, a momentary tingle
In the long cold aeons of stone
These stones have seen the world take shape
If I can ask the right questions
They will tell me many things
The voices told me that asking questions of rocks was futile.

I asked him anyway
About the voices in my head.
He said that he never heard things
Like that anymore.
I used to, he said. Before I found out about stones.

He offered to ask the stones for me,
And after he threw them he said
That stones never heard voices,
And you could not be sure what
They were saying sometimes,
But that these ones seemed to like me
And that was the best sign of all.
Keep doing what you're doing he said
Already crouching over his papers.
I left him to his rocks and his drawing and went on my way.

Next I found a firework maker
His hands were grey with the dust of alchemy
And his hair was grey and standing on its surprised ends
Also he had no eyebrows
He said: I am the medium between the light
And the hand clapping joy of the child
I am the air that feeds the burning spark
But at the same time protects the ears
Of the watching crowd as they stand well back
(further back please ladies and gentleman)
Half scared and all enthralled
I know the secrets of the red dust,
And the blue dust, and the yellow powder,
And the small pile of charcoal at the end of the night.

My best friend is fire
In all its lively warmth
And its undead unyielding hunger.

I asked him where his eyebrows went
And he said that you lose many things for love.
He said he used to hear voices too,
but they went away around the same time as the eyebrows.

He offered to light a firework for me
To guide me on my way,
And it when the fuse burnt down
It was a rocket, screaming high into the sky
Like pure joy unsheathed and getting lost among the stars
I thanked the firework maker, and followed it
Wondering if all stars were born of fireworks
    and the people who loved them.

Next I sat down by a river
I did not know what I wanted
But I had been walking for so long.
It was quiet by the river, and the grasses
Started telling me their secrets.
One seed
At a time.

Things kept floating by on the river
Castles in the mist,
And abandoned shopping trolleys.
Witches in tea cups and
Jesus' face in a slice of potato.
I did not know what to do next,
But that did not seem to matter anymore
Like a dream upon waking when the logic melts away
As if it was but candle wax all along.
I asked the voices inside me what I should do,
    but there was no reply.

feather down

Currawong squats
On the clothesline again
Swallows unripe grape again
Grape again
Agape again
Hops to the grapevine again
Unripe gulp again
Grape again
Grape
Again
Squat hop rustle again
Gulp again
Stares at me with
Mad gold eye.

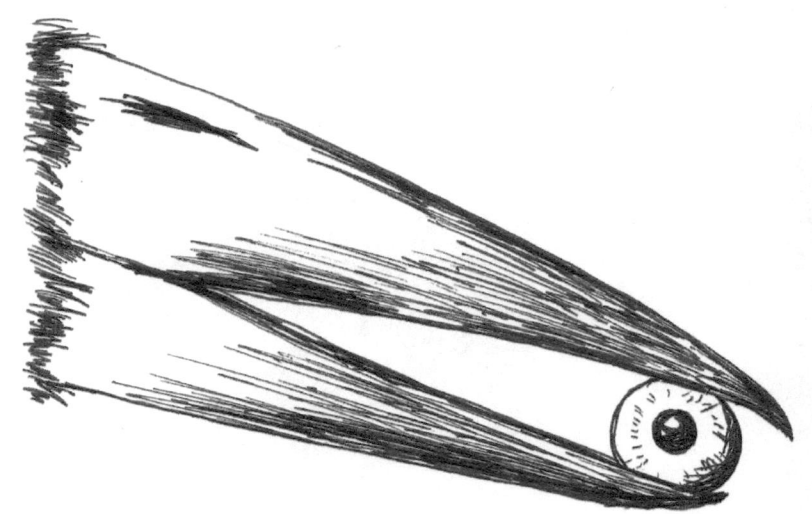

Currawong eats baby rats
If it can get them
Baby rats
Tiny soft
Baby grapes
Baby feijoa flowers
Sweet off the tree
Currawong eats
Baby birds
When it can
Young quivering bundle
Again
Gulp again
Spins feather down
To gold again

Gold for its mad, bright eye.

notes: *incomplete performance history*

"Frost Hollow" was written for an audio collaboration with Reuben Ingall, release forthcoming. This poem takes a line from the play *You're safe till 2024*, David Finnegan 2019.

"The Catchment" was first performed at Canberra Slamboree, February 2019. This poem was previously published as an online video, February 2020 https://youtu.be/BS4xV_uKuD8

"Wild Horses" was first performed at Canberra Slamboree April 2019. This poem was previously published as an online video, February 2020 https://youtu.be/IK6yJDI8XQ8

"The Stone Witch" was written and performed for Queensland Poetry Festival as part of the solo show *Anabranch*, August 2018.

"Erasing Geography" was performed in collaboration with musical group Super Rats, at Poets for Breakfast, May 2016.

"Cleopatra" was previously published as "Lady Kim of Belconnen" in *Hold it Close*, Pilcrow Press 2015 and in *Crace: Walk the Line*, exhibition catalogue for the Crace Field Study, Australian National University 2014. Performed at the exhibition opening for the Crace Field Study, November 2014.

"Time Makes Deserts" was first performed for the Australian Poetry Slam finals, October 2015. Recording available at https://youtu.be/Q-jM_ZP1E0o

"Breathe" was first published in *Meniscus* vol 2, Issue 2 2014.

"Driving Straight Through" was first performed at Bloody Lips, November 2014.

"Their Summer Call" was written with musical collaboration by Callum Henshaw, first performed at A Song, The World to Come, March 2017.

"Recipe for Fire (again)" was written as a duet with Raphael Kabo. This poem was previously published as a sound file, June 2018 https://soundcloud.com/lucubratory/recipe-for-fire-again

"Unwelcome Warmth" was first published in *Seizure*, August 2015.

"Voices" was performed with musical improvisation by Fossil Rabbit, at Bad!Slam!No!Biscuit, February 2015 and Gorgeous Mortar, September 2015.

"Feather Down" was first performed at Canberra Slamboree, February 2017.

about us

A book is not a solo project. My deepest gratitude to Caren Florance, publisher and typography witch, who invited me to do this project with her Thanks to Helani Laisk for creating the perfect illustrations for this book, and for being a dream to work with. An ocean of thanks to Raphael Kabo, for editing my words, for being with me on this journey since that first midnight discussion about books.

My thanks go to members of my poetry coven for making poetry about more than words: Aaron Kirby, Ellie Malbon, Fiona McLeod, Jacqui Malins, Marls Filmer-Sankey, Melinda Smith and Shane Strange. For always being there, thank you to Clair Boyer and Cal Henshaw.

Zoe Anderson is a performance poet who is fascinated by ecology, place and creating new folklore for a changing world. She is a seasoned performer, having featured at festivals including You Are Here festival, Poetry on the Move, and the Queensland Poetry Festival. Zoe is one of the organisers of Slamboree, the world's best scout themed poetry slam. Zoe comes from Canberra, which is Ngunnawal country. *Under the Skin of the World* is her first poetry collection.
FB/INSTA @zoeandherwords

Helani Laisk is a Canberra-born multi-media artist with an interest in human behaviour. She completed a Bachelor of Visual Arts (Honours) at the ANU School of Art, majoring in printmedia and drawing, and has since exhibited and participated in arts festivals around the country. Grounded by a practice that encompasses drawing, animation, print, textiles and interactive/participatory installation, Helani forms surrealist imaginings about how we relate to each other and the world, using visual metaphor and personification as a way of exploring the complexities of emotional states and the links between fantasy and lived human experience.
INSTA @h3l4n1

Caren Florance is happy to claim the title 'type witch', although she prefers 'type harpy'. She has a complex, collaborative relationship with poetry and enjoys the wrestle of containing it in a page, using a mix of old and new technologies. Big thanks to Recent Work Press for being a flexible publishing playground! Caren lives in Canberra and works at a few universities.

http://carenflorance.com   INSTA @ampersandduck

Under the skin of the world
Recent Work Press + Ampersand Duck
Canberra, Australia

ISBN: 978-0-64868-537-1

Copyright © Zoe Anderson 2020

All rights reserved. This book is copyright. Except for private study, research, criticism or reviews as permitted under the Copyright Act, no part of this book may be reproduced stored in a retrieval system, or transmitted in any form by any means without prior written permission. Enquiries should be addressed to the publisher.

Design & layout: Caren Florance
carenflorance.com

Typeset in various sizes of Baskerville. Cover is set in Mrs Eaves.

Cover image and illustrations: Helani Laisk

recentworkpress.com

www.ingramcontent.com/pod-product-compliance
Lightning Source LLC
Chambersburg PA
CBHW020329010526
44107CB00054B/2045